CO

BORNEO - Sabah, Brunei & Sarawak

On arrival in the Philippines visitors must have proof of an onward flight-useful to know beforehand! I didn't!

Those in the queue behind me were somewhat amused when I was offered a list of cheap flights. 'Where do you want to go next?' 'I don't know. What have you got?' I settled for Kota Kinabalu, Sabah, all for the princely sum of £12.

30 days later, as we flew over the island, the peak of majestic Mt Kinabalu rose out of the clouds...it was higher than the plane!

I decided that my first task on landing would be to see the rest of the mountain-the bit below the clouds. I caught a local bus which took me through some glorious scenery to a majestic rock face rising out of the jungle, with occasional gaps in the cloud giving brief, enticing glimpses of its peak.

My aim was to then travel by various forms of local transport in a SW direction to Kuching in Sarawak, with possible detours into the interior along some of the steep, wide river valleys that run down from the wild, mountainous centre of the island-home to tribes that used to live by hunting in the jungle with blow pipes & still live in communal longhouses

At Beauport, 90km. south of Kota Kinabalu, I found a quaint little railway following the course of the Padas River inland to the small town of Tenom. Two metal boxes on wheels pulled by an engine, it could only be described as a 'bone shaker'...

05/11/2018 13:35

The journey offers splendid, close-up views of the river

05/11/2018 08:40

05/11/2018 09:04

Along the way it picked up friendly, smiling people & dropped them at idyllic clearings in the jungle, where they often lined the track & waved me goodbye as the train departed

On the way back, taking a seat at the front of the train by a conveniently placed window, I found that I was sat next to the driver in what can only be described as the Observation Platform.

05/11/2018 13:53

Like a lot of youngsters from my generation, I found myself as a young boy wanting to be an engine driver! Something to do with living a nomadic existence & being In charge of your own destiny, I guess.

I remember once, around the age of 10, along with my father, gazing enthralled through a partition window into the cab of one of the new diesel trains that ran along the Calder Valley Line near my home in England.

The driver looked round & invited us inside. Not quite believing we were in such a hallowed place, he then asked me if I'd like to guide the train, it's 3 coaches & full complement of passengers, into the next station!

He showed me how to slowly move a lever back & forth &, after some initial doubts on my part had been overcome, I brought the train smoothly to a halt at Mytholmroyd Station, the other occupants of the train being non the wiser.

We replayed events again over supper that evening, not quite believing what had taken place that afternoon. A far cry from today's health & safety society where I would have been met with a locked door & a NO ENTRY sign!

On this occasion I sat content, enjoying the view as we arrived back at Beaufort

My next destination was Brunei. Arriving by sea, including a hair raising speedboat trip via the tax haven of Labaun Island, you pass some of the oil wells which make the Sultan of Brunei one of the richest men in the world.

His country is an unusual place with a ban on alcohol & little or no nightlife, where female pop singers appear on TV performing with their headscarves on.   Like a lot of affluent parts of the world, such as Dubai, Kuwait & Hong Kong, it runs on cheap Indian & Filipino labour, & these people usually turn out to be the most welcoming & friendliest of the people there.

True to form, as I stood at a bus stop near the ferry port looking lost, two strangers approached & offered to guide me to the city centre...Filipino workers.

The city has well manicured with modern roads & buildings. My favorite part was the old, traditional, coloured market by the river, where families arrived by boat to do their shopping

Moving on to Miri in Sarawak, it was Saturday night & every European worker in Brunei seemed to have crossed over the border to drink & party, including a group of Irish oil workers, having an early St.Patricks Day knees up. This Saturday night excursion is evidently a regular event.

Down the coast at Sibu, I found a local ferry service travelling up the mighty Rajang River to Kaput...

Barges full of logs travel downstream....

Local tribes live along the river bank & in days gone by, climbing the rapids further upstream would put you in danger of encountering the headhunting tribes that inhabited this region.

As it was, a man ran to the river bank & started jumping up & down, waving his arms & beating his chest in a kind of tribal dance when he saw me on the boat!

However, he had a big grin on his face...I waved back!!

The following morning brought another hair raising boat journey. Following the Rajang downstream this time, the destination was Kuching. The 200 seater express speed boat made good time on the river's smooth surface....

...& then shot straight out into the open sea, where it was tossed about by the waves!!

On arrival in Kuching it was a heart warming sight to see Orang Utans at the local rescue centre.

Here they are taken care of, then released back into the wild.

There's nothing to prevent them wandering away from the area, but they choose to stick around, taking advantage of a twice daily feed, which is the best time to see them.....

Nearby is an area where Pitcher Plants grow

These fascinating carnivores collect water. Their prey, small insects & the like, crawl inside for a drink, then the top shuts & they are trapped & digested!

At the Kuching Cultural Village you can experience tribal life in traditional houses & be entertained by local dance & music

Taking a walk to the nearby coast reveals something of the wild nature of the island

My journey across Borneo was the start of a long, circuitous journey home. As I'd stepped out of my guest house in Kota Kinabalu on the first morning, locals were looking up at the Solar Eclipse...an auspicious start to a journey, I thought!

One of the many interesting things I find travelling around Asia is the variety of English language newspapers & their different slants on world news. The Bangkok Post, Times of India, China Daily & best of all here, the Borneo Bulletin! That morning's edition told of how the local Dayak tribe had been performing a ritual ceremony 'to ensure the eclipse doesn't go on for too long'! Thus I was able to confidently prepare for my journey home...

Back in Kuching, at the end of the day I found people enjoying one of their favorite pastimes - watching the sunset

Returning to Borneo on a sunny day a couple of years later, Kota
Kinabalu provided a colourful welcome

This time I took the bus to Sandakan, formerly the old British colonial town of Elopura, Kota Kinabalu being once named Jesselton. I was soon reacquainting myself with majestic views of Mt. Kinabalu on the way. This is Malaysia's highest mountain

02/11/2018 05:14

At Sandakan I enjoyed afternoon tea in the English Tea House, an old colonial outpost complete with croquet lawn. I asked about the possibility of having a game, but was disappointed to find that the ball was missing! The British Empire has well & truly ended! However, excellent views of the surrounding area & coastline were to be had from it's elevated position above the town

27/10/2018

On display were various artefacts & accessories from a bye-gone age, including this old iron, which would have been filled with red hot coals before use.

I remembered seeing a similar one still in use in Madras, India, sometime in the 1980's.

Next door stands Newlands, the former home of American author Agnes Keith, famous for her autobiographical accounts of life in Borneo under Japanese occupancy during the Second World War. Sandakan was captured in January 1942 & Europeans were rounded up & held on Pulau Berhala, a large island nearby. The house was taken over by the Commandant of the notorious Japanese POW Camp situated just outside the town, Captain Susumi Hoshijima.

Anges bravely took part in resistance activities against the Japanese & was a prominent member of Sandakan's Underground Assistance Group.

30

Also in the town stands the dilapidated Sandakhan Recreational Club, formed in 1902 - now another interesting reminder it's bye-gone past. A multi-racial establishment, it was the first stopping off place for vsitors to Sandakan..

In his book 'Borneo:Stealer of Hearts', Oscar Cook talks of 'Steamers of the world, from Australia, Manila, China & the East Indies arrive....their presence breathes a wider, freer life felt in every corner of the town.
Here today & gone tomorrow, a traveller of repute, a great journalist, a naturalist, an opium smuggler all pass through here & come to the club; they tell their stories & shed their personalities, leaving behind them some subtle contact with the world'.

Still in use in 2004, according to an old guidebook I found in the town, but it's doors finally closed sometime between then & now

The only downside to the town is the litter that washes up on the sea front.

Plastic bottles, carrier bags & other debris are washed up daily on the recently built seawall, detracting from the splendid views that the walkway commands.

However, local people are becoming aware of the problem & the need to up clean up similar areas in other parts of Asia & hopefully this will happen here too in the near future...

33

Nearby, fishermen sort through the morning's catch & the Infinity
pool of a nearby hotel gives an interesting snapshot of the bay

At Taman Rimba, on the site of the previously mentioned POW
Camp, there now stand the tranquil Australian Memorial gardens...

Commemorating the death of approximately 2,400 Australian & British prisoners of war held here, memories of their stay still lay scattered around.

The steam from the camp boiler helped produce it's electricity. In order to obtain sufficient voltage to operate a secret radio the prisoners had made, the local operator of the plant, Chan Ping, helped by increasing the power supply in the evenings!

Prisoners were tasked with building an airstrip for the town. One day the Japanese produced this mechanical excavator to help speed up the work. After one days use it was sabotaged by a prisoner & never worked again!

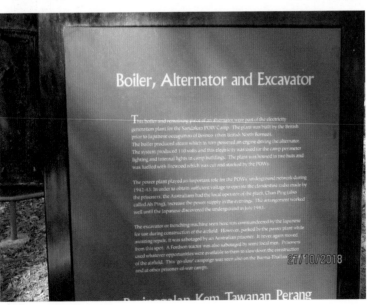

Boiler, Alternator and Excavator

This boiler and remaining piece of an alternator were part of the electricity generation plant for the Sandakan POW Camp. The plant was built by the British prior to Japanese occupation of Borneo (then British North Borneo).
The boiler produced steam which in turn powered an engine driving the alternator. The system produced 110 volts and this electricity was used for the camp perimeter lighting and internal lights in camp buildings. The plant was housed in two huts and was fuelled with firewood which was cut and stacked by the POWs.

The power plant played an important role for the POWs' underground network during 1942-43. In order to obtain sufficient voltage to operate the clandestine radio made by the prisoners, the Australians had the local operator of the plant, Chin Ping (also called Ah Ping), increase the power supply in the evenings. The arrangement worked well until the Japanese discovered the underground in July 1943.

The excavator or trenching machine seen here was commandeered by the Japanese for use during construction of the airfield. However, parked by the power plant while awaiting repair, it was sabotaged by an Australian prisoner. It never again moved from this spot. A Fordson tractor was also sabotaged by some local men. Prisoners used whatever opportunities were available to them to slow down the construction of the airfield. This 'go-slow' campaign was seen also on the Burma-Thailand and at other prisoner-of-war camps.

Peninggalan Kem Tawanan Perang

37

Towards the end of the war the emaciated figures that had
survived Japanese brutality were ordered out of the camp on three
Death Marches to the towns of Kundasan & Ranau (shown in the
following two pictures) over 100 kms away in the mountainous
jungle nr. Mt.Kinabalu.
Not one of them reached there!

There were only six survivors out of the 1,000 sick & weak men
who set off - & they survived by escaping into the jungle, where
they were fed & sheltered by local people.
One of the survivors recalled being marched out of the camp to the
road outside — turning left, they knew, would have led them to the
harbour & the hope of freedom — they were forced to turn right!

By coincidence, the following day's Borneo Post carried a story of the death, at the age of 105, of the last remaining local worker, forced by the Japanese to help clear their path through the jungle...

Last known Death March track cutter dies

Kan Yaw Chong

KOTA KINABALU: Tuaty Akau, 105, the last known Death March track cutter who hacked the mid track from Bauto through thick jungle, has died.

Tuaty (**pic**) died last Monday (Oct 29), which ironically coincided with his birthday.

Hailed from Kg Buis, about 8km from Bauto, near Telupid, Tuaty joined his father-in-law who was recruited by the Japanese to cut the trail to mid track passage ready to march hundreds of Australian and British prisoners of war from Sandakan to Ranau.

Tuaty had told Daily Express in an investigative interview he hated the job because the dense jungle made hacking tough and the Japanese guards expected hard work.

"One time my fellow track cutter stopped for a cigarette and was hit on the head with a rod," he said.

He also remembered seeing weak prisoners passing and out of pity offered rice but was scolded by the guards.

See Page 2, Col. 2

41

Local people are also honoured at the memorial gardens. This nine year old girl, named Balabiu, gave food to the starving prisoners on the march, at great risk to her young self

Nine year-old Balabiu gave food to starving POW's on the Death Marches. Here she is listening to a recording made of her story with Ranau missionary Trevor White and Major H.W.S Jackson

Balabiu ketika berusia sembilan tahun memberi makanan kepadapara tawanan perang yang kelaparan dalam Kawat-kawat Maut. Dalam gambar ini ia sedang mendengar rakaman ceritanya bersama mubaligh Ranau Trevor... Major H.W.S Jackson

27/10/2018

Ranau is now renowned for its popular Sabah Tea & the nearby Poring Hot Springs - a nice, relaxing place to visit.

Here you can plonk yourself down in your own, individual outdoor tub & balance between hot & cold taps to find your own perfect temperature, the spa waters having health giving qualities

And in Kundasan, this street art now makes for interesting reading

Many visitors these days are drawn to the area by the Sepilok OrangUtan Sanctuary.

Here, rescued members of the threatened species, some orphaned, are gradually taught how to survive in the wild, with the aim of eventually returning them to their natural habitat.

There are also Conservation Centres for Sun Bears & Probiscus Monkeys nearby, while insect life abounds

Browsing through my shopping list one morning before setting off for the local market in Sandakan, the word CROCS stood out in bold letters!

Handy for swimming & snorkelling – you can walk painlessly along rocky shores & the water drains out of the holes in them when you enter the water.

The phrase 'be careful what you wish for' immediately sprang to mind!

It's not unusual to see pairs of steely, focused eyes pointing out of the water in the rivers of this part of the world!

Arriving at the Kinabatangan River, what at first looked like a log on the opposite bank turned out to be a sizeable, fully grown male of the species, dozing in the early afternoon sun!

I'd arrived there by local bus from Sandakan as it looked like a convenient stopping off spot, the road to Tahad Ladu crossing the river at this point by way of this iron suspension bridge

Friendly teachers & students from the Universiti Teknologi MARA (UiTM) Sabah Branch, were also at the river, staying at the Kopel Miso Walai Homestead, where trips along the river & into the jungle can be arranged, conservation being very much at the forefront of their efforts

The group from the university were studying tourism, a field trip here to the 'Amazon of the East' being an important part of their course.

Boyd, Silverina & Christy were quick to show me their special jungle shoes - rubber, waterproof, cheap (£1) light to carry, known locally as 'Borneo Addidas'. Christy's, on the left, even came complete with Go Fast stripes, as she proudly pointed out

Taking a sunset trip myself in a small canoe, I sat entranced as the boatman pointed out kingfishers, hornbills, eagles, small colourful birds & an owl, as long-tailed monkeys swung through exotic vegetation on the riverbank, while in the water the occasional crocodile lazily observed our leisurely passing!

As mentioned, the road south from the Kinabatangan River leads to the coastal town of Lahad Datu.

On 23 September 1985, there was a stand off here when 15-20 armed foreign pirates from the neighbouring Philippines landed, killing at least 21 people and injuring 11 others.

Piracy has been commonplace in this area for over 200 years. No skull, crossbones & cutlasses these days - modern day pirates use speedboats & automatic rifles.

There were rumours that foreign tourists have occasionally been kidnapped along the peaceful looking sea front at Sandakan where I'd recently walked - ransoms put on their heads to buy their freedom.

Wise to research & remember that even in the most tranquil of places there may be are isolated trouble spots.

On the way back to Kota K, unable to resist the temptation to explore the area around <u>Mt. Kinabalu</u> further, I made my way to Jungle Jack's Backpacker's Hostel, situated conveniently at it's base.

From this delightful, friendly, ramshackled haven you can sit out on the balcony for hours, observing the ever changing views.

As the morning mist rolls over the nearby hills, it often obscures the view, but soon opens up again to reveal everything in a new light

The area was the scene of a devastating earthquake on the morning of June 5th 2015 that altered the shape of the peak. 18 climbers & guides perished, along with around 60 people in surrounding villages, or so the press reported.

Locals told me that the figure was more like 200!

03/11/2018 05:59

I always like to have a good reading book on the go when I'm travelling, to the extent that I often feel a little lost & disorientated when I don't! Ideally, content will be related to the area I'm in & often furnishing me with ideas of where to go next. A few days later after leaving Borneo, finding myself bookless, another one of those strange coincidences took place.

Chatting to a friendly Westerner at a bar in Ayutthaya, Thailand, I asked him if he had any books that he happened to have finished reading.

The following evening he turned up with a copy of 'Return to a Dark Age', the Story of Billy Young, a young Australian who aged just 15 years, lied about his age in order to join the Australian Army in World War 2. He was sent to Singapore, captured by the Japanese, eventually ending up in the same POW camp that I'd just visited in Sandakan!

The story of the sabotaged mechanical excavator & the camp boiler were all described in the book.

And finally I leave you with some of my other favorite pictures from my two visits to the rather interesting island of Borneo

05/11/2018 13:59

62

65

Health & Safety has even reached this remote part of the world...

HUTAN SIMPAN SIBUGA
PUBLIC NOTICE ON SAFETY IN SIBUGA FOREST RESERVE

1. Kami telah berusaha untuk memastikan Taman ini adalah selamat sepanjang masa, walaubagaimanapun kami tidak menjamin dapat mengelakkan berlakunya kejadian dan kemalangan yang tidak di ingini.
   As much as we want to keep this Forest Reserve Park safe at all times, we cannot guarantee that untoward incidents will not happen.

2. Sebagai Hutan Simpan, Taman ini mempunyai pelbagai bentuk hidupan biologi yang boleh atau tidak mengancam keselamatan pengguna-pengguna.
   Being a Forest Reserve, this Park has a range of biological life forms that may or may not threaten the safety of users.

3. Ini adalah termasuk: Ular seperti Ular Tedung dan Ular Sawa, Biawak, Lebah, Penyengat dan Tebuan, Kalajengking, dahan jatuh dan sebagainya.
   These include: snakes such as Cobras and Pythons, Giant Monitor Lizards, Bees, Wasps and Hornets, Scorpions, falling branches etc.

4. Semasa cuaca hujan, laluan penjalan kaki boleh menjadi licin disebabkan tompokan lumut dan sebagainya.
   During rainy weather, the footpaths may also be slippery in spots as they accumulate mould etc.

5. Dari masa ke semasa, penceroboh dan penjenayah mungkin akan memasuki kawasan ini tanpa pengetahuan pihak kami.
   From time to time, Deviants and Miscreants may also slip in outside our notice.

6. Maka dengan itu, kami tidak akan bertanggungjawab ke atas keselamatan pengguna-pengguna dan risiko memasuki hutan simpan ini adalah atas tanggungjawab mereka sendiri.
   We are therefore not responsible for the safety of users and they enter this Forest Reserve at their own risk.

Dengan itu sila berhati-hati dan sentiasa peka semasa berada di dalam Hutan Simpan.
Please therefore be mindful and sensible at all times while in this reserve.

Thanks for reading & if you've enjoyed this book on Borneo you might like to try one of my other travel books in the 'Let Loose Again' series for the following countries – Vietnam, Laos, Borneo, Indonesia (Bali, Sumatra & Java), Philippines, Cambodia, India, Hong Kong & England - also available on Amazon

Printed in Poland
by Amazon Fulfillment
Poland Sp. z o.o., Wrocław